# FREE
# COLLEGE

# FREE COLLEGE

## HOW GRADUATES EARN THE MOST SCHOLARSHIP MONEY

For Families of Pre-K through High School Students

## ELIZABETH WALLACE

LOS ANGELES, CALIFORNIA

©ElizabethWallace
@ElizaWallace27
roadtofreecollege.com

For information about special discounts on bulk purchases to schools and other non-profit organizations, please contact us at freecollegeinfo@earthlink.net.

This publication is a creative work fully protected by all applicable rights. All rights reserved. No portion of the book may be reproduced or transmitted in any form or by any means, electronic or mechanical, including fax, photocopy or recording, or any other information storage or retrieval system by anyone. This book may not be reproduced in its entirely without written permission of the author.

ISBN 978-0-9911912-2-2
Book Design: Connie Shaw, egrafics.com
Cover Design: Bruce Berglund, Berglund Advertising Design

Although the information collected for this guide is accurate and the recommendations contained therein have been proven to help students obtain free scholarship and grant money for college, the level of success of any individual using this information may vary. Therefore, the publisher and author disclaim any implied warranty of suitability for any particular purpose.

The strategies and advice contained in this book may not be appropriate for every situation or person. The degree to which an individual follows these recommendations and applies for scholarships or grants in a timely manner will play a significant role in exactly how much scholarship and/or grant money is received, if any. Other variables include: whether or not an applicant has fulfilled all A—G requirements, completed Honors, AP and/or IB courses, has a high GPA, how much money is available at the time and how many others apply for specific individual grants and scholarships. Names of students appearing in this book have been changed to ensure their privacy.

# DEDICATION

For my James Monroe High School counselor who taught me a valuable lesson early in life. "You can out work smart, but you can't out smart lazy." It made all the difference.

# PRAISE FOR FREE COLLEGE

"A much needed book depicting eye-opening methods easily employed by parents and students to maximize scholarships covering college tuition and expenses."

—*Shelley Schuber, Author*

"This book should be available to parents before their children enter school. A perfect handbook for student success."

—*Jeanette A. Frath, B.A., Psychology; M.A., Social Science*

"Addresses one of the most important topics of our time… eliminating college debt! Clearly and concisely, in easy-to-read steps, how to accomplish this."

—*Kathryn Beckmann Khalifa, B.A., ML, Former Reference Librarian*

Avoid post college debt! Fantastic tips for getting to college! Plan ahead for college."

—*Diane Hearne, Author*

"Most people aren't aware of what's available. This book increases awareness, step by step. Much needed information for the college process in a concise and thorough reference book. A college funding Bible!"

—*Susan Suhr, B.A., M.B.A.*

"The information this book contains will be vital to any student unable to personally finance a full university course of instruction."

—*Al Jacobs, B.S., US Naval Academy,
B.S., Civil Engineering, B.S. & M.S., Chemistry*

"Instead of paying full tuition to put four daughters through college, I would have loved to know the information provided in *Free College* while our daughters were growing up. It would have made a tremendous difference to us financially. *Free College* could improve the financial security of millions of families."

—*Deborah Carr, Retired Realtor,
Author of Retirement Planning Secrets for a Happy Future*

"It's much needed information for kids starting high school. It could guide their study habits that could help them enter college."

—*Mary Jo West, B.S., M.S., ASCP*

"Ms. Wallace has a genuine passion for her subject and a knack for incorporating many other lessons/advice that I have taken with me to college (and will keep with me forever)."

*—Jessica W., Former Student*

"A significant lesson I learned was that the best ways to prepare for the future is to plan the future."

*—Angelica B., Former Student*

"Ms. Wallace has a wealth of ideas and the 'know how' and energy to get the job done."

*—Lynn M., Former Student*

# HOW YOU CAN MAKE A DIFFERENCE
*The Starfish Story*
*Adapted from "Star Thrower", by Loren Eiseley*

A young man was walking along the ocean after a storm and saw a beach on which thousands of starfish had washed ashore. He saw an older man walking slowly and stooping every so often, picking up one starfish after another and tossing each one into the sea.

"Why are you throwing starfish into the ocean?" he asked.

"Because the sun is up, and the tide is out. If I don't throw them into the water, they'll die."

"But, there are thousands of starfish along the beach. You can't possibly save enough to make a difference."

The old man listened, bent down to pick up another starfish and threw it into the sea.

"It made a difference to that one."

*Give a copy of this book to anyone you know with Pre-K through High School aged children.*

# CAREER & TECHNICAL READINESS

*"The biggest adventure you can take is to live the life of your dreams."*
*Oprah Winfrey*

Although this book contains strategies adopted by successful college scholarship winners, it will also benefit those who choose a different path. Students who implement these practices will develop the work habits, character traits, interpersonal skills and life balance which will help them become valuable employees, freelancers, business owners and members of society. Acquiring the skill set contained within this book will benefit all students. As American entrepreneur, inventor and founder of Apple, Steve Jobs, once said, "Your time is limited, so don't waste it living someone else's life."

# ACKNOWLEGEMENTS

*"Many hands make light work."*
*John Heywood*

Although I don't have the power or authority to eliminate college tuition, I do possess valuable information which can help students graduate debt free. It would have remained in my file cabinet and mind, were it not for the very effective harassment of my sister, Shirley Jewett.

My friend, Debbie Carr played a significant role in my actually finishing my book. Her not so gentle questions at our monthly lunches embarrassed me into bringing the writing to a close. Connie Shaw is a patient and tech savvy friend who put up with my frustration when I couldn't convince my computer to do what I needed done. I don't know how she put up with me.

I also owe a debt of gratitude to my local writers' group for their suggestions, questions and editing skills. They helped make this book user friendly and personal. I'm grateful as well to Al Jacobs who wrote the insightful foreword. Everyone who benefits from reading *Free College* should join me in thanking these people, all of whom helped make it possible.

# TABLE OF CONTENTS

1. DO MORE. BE MORE. GET MORE.   25
2. TAKE ENRICHMENT CLASSES   33
3. TAKE MUSIC LESSONS   41
4. USE VISUAL AIDS   49
5. EAT BREAKFAST DAILY   59
6. START LOOKING EARLY   67
7. GET NOTICED   75
8. JOIN STUDY GROUPS   83
9. FOCUS   91
10. COMPLETE EVERY ASSIGNMENT   99
11. ASK QUESTIONS   107
12. BEFRIEND COMPETITIVE PEOPLE   115
13. COMMIT TO EXTRACURRICULAR ACTIVITIES   123
14. DINE AS A FAMILY   131
15. FIND A MENTOR   139
16. MAKE WISE CHOICES   147
17. FOLLOW THROUGH   155
18. TIMELINE   163

# ABOUT THE AUTHOR

Elizabeth Wallace has been a successful language teacher, adjunct community college professor, author and public speaker for more than four decades. Trained as a teacher of French, German and English, after receiving her BA from California State University Fullerton, she built award winning foreign language programs in several public high schools. As an academic elective teacher, she learned to supply added value to her programs in order for them to grow. This resulted in winning several prestigious awards.

She was recruited by the Goethe Institute to author a book showing German teachers in the U.S. how to build a successful German Program like hers in public schools. She has been a sought after presenter at local and national conferences to speak on this topic and others. In addition, she has been active in civic affairs in her community and was appointed City Commissioner where she served for nine years. Ms. Wallace then earned an MBA from Redlands University and taught business administration in the public and private sectors in the U.S. and abroad.

Ms. Wallace, while no longer teaching students full time, has now taken on the even more challenging role within the education community of writing curriculum, consulting, and training teachers and trainers. She is staying involved with education by writing *Free College*, maintaining an online presence at roadtofreecollege.com and encouraging students to graduate from college debt free. Far too many students are graduating from college with crushing debt. Elizabeth Wallace intends to help students become the ideal college scholarship and grant applicant, so they can earn more free cash for college and begin their careers debt free.

# FOREWORD

In an earlier era, the cost of a higher education fit into the budgets of the least affluent among us. Things are not quite the same these days. A university degree can cost a fortune. Room, board, fees and tuition at Northwestern University in Evanston, Illinois, now runs $62,500 per year. And for this, after four years, you get a diploma which may or may not entitle you to a job. Richard Vedder, an Ohio University economist and expert on college costs declared: "Colleges and universities may be the least cost-effective institutions in the United States."

It goes without saying that if you can finance your higher education at someone else's expense, that's the way to go. The most effective way to locate a fairy godmother is through a scholarship. They're available, but it takes time and effort, but most of all it takes knowledgeable guidance—which is the subject of this book.

The alternative routes to your sought after higher education are much less desirable. Today's most conventional—though perhaps most hazardous—method is the federal student loan program. They're usually easy to qualify for and require no cosigner. A recent article's title tells the story: "Student Debt a Growing Monster." At $1.2 trillion, student loans are second only to mortgages as a source of consumer debt. Nearly 71 percent of college graduates floated loans, with the average now $35,000 in hock. I unequivocally disapprove of obtaining a loan to attend college.

I'll conclude with this final thought. Education is truly the royal road to advancement. Those who choose their profession with thoughtfulness, devote their attention to the course of study, and wisely avoid encumbering themselves with debt they cannot service, will find their lives to be far smoother.

Al Jacobs has been a professional investor for over four decades. His credentials include degrees from the U.S. Naval Academy, Rensselaer Polytechnic Institute, and UC Irvine, as well as a Real Estate Certificate from UC Berkeley and a CPM designation from the Institute of Real Estate Management. He draws on his extensive expertise in real estate, mortgage, and securities investments to counsel on how to invest wisely and spend prudently. He's the author of *Roadway to Prosperity—A Practical Guide to Wealth Accumulation*. You may view his weekly *Straight Talk from Al Jacobs* and his monthly newsletter, *On the Money Trail*, by visiting his website www.roadwaytoprosperity.com.

# 1

## DO MORE. BE MORE. GET MORE.

*"Be willing to do today what others won't,
so you can live tomorrow like others don't."*

John C. Maxwell

Have you ever wondered why some high school graduates are awarded massive amounts of free cash for college in the form of Full-Ride Scholarships or grants while other deserving students receive peanuts? So have I. **If you would like to learn the secret of receiving more free cash for college, read on.** You'll discover the specific behaviors that have allowed many worthy students to graduate, degree in hand, debt free.

I wrote *Free College* to help students earn a university education without accumulating debt. When I first began teaching, few of my students had plans to pursue higher education. I decided to do what I could to change that. Whenever someone started a sentence with, "If I graduate from high school," I interrupted with, "You mean, when you go to college." Eventually the tide changed. I started hearing, "After I graduate from college…"

As motivation for my freshmen, sophomore and junior students, early each January, I put up a large poster in the front of my foreign language classroom. On the top I had written "Senior Post-Graduation Plans" in bold letters. Each senior was urged to record what he or she intended to do upon high school graduation. The first year, about one-third wrote the name of a college or university, one-third the name of a community college or trade school and the remainder wrote either "military" or "undecided". Fairly quickly these ratios changed. As I continued to push, eventually all seniors began listing colleges and universities plus their chosen field of study, first name and last name initial for all to see.

One evening while watching a television show on financial matters, I noticed a viewer mentioned she was still paying off her student loan debt. She was in her forties. I was appalled. I investigated and soon realized many college students graduate with a degree and a massive amount of debt.

I began to encourage my students to select the least expensive accredited university they could find that would provide the education they needed for the field of their choice. **I also preached scholarships and grants over student loans.** During the last half of my teaching career, all my graduating seniors not only went to college after high school, but also received some form of scholarship or grant to help pay tuition.

Two years before I retired, while congratulating one of my students upon her notification of being a Bill and Melinda Gates Millennium Scholarship (Full-Ride for Life) recipient, I wondered why the very qualified student sitting next to her wasn't also a winner. I resolved to figure out why some students are awarded a small amount of cash for college, while others receive a Full-Ride. I decided I would survey students, look into their records and ask a great deal of questions to determine if there were any differences which might result in these outcomes.

I followed through with this decision. I spent several years researching hundreds of high school graduates who received scholarships for college. Some earned very little scholarship or grant money, while others earned a Full-Ride. Many in this substantial study group were interviewed, far more filled out surveys and questionnaires. Still others wrote long explanations of their experiences while growing up. The real world information I gathered became the foundation of this book.

After years of research, I discovered a pattern of behaviors. Those who perform more of certain specific actions become more of what colleges are looking for and receive more free cash. **Students who develop particular habits transform themselves into the ideal scholarship recipient.** In the following chapters, you'll find these habits listed and explained. You'll see how students who practiced these habits diligently were later awarded Full-Ride Scholarships to the universities of their choice. Those who were less successful in following these principles received less money.

German writer and statesman Johann Wolfgang von Goethe is often quoted as saying, the moment one definitely commits oneself, Providence moves too. Full-Ride Scholarship winners know Goethe was right. Action has magic, power and grace within it. In this book you'll learn which actions are most likely to lead to earning more free cash for college.

## CHAPTER 1 - ACTION PLAN: (Parents)

Make a list of all strengths, talents, positive personality traits and interests of each of your children (separate page for each child, if possible); update this list every six months.

_____
_____
_____
_____
_____
_____
_____
_____
_____
_____
_____
_____
_____
_____
_____
_____
_____
_____
_____
_____
_____
_____
_____
_____

# FREE COLLEGE

Do More. Be More. Get More.

# FREE COLLEGE

# 2

# TAKE ENRICHMENT CLASSES

*"Education is the key to unlock the golden door of freedom."*
*George Washington Carver*

One hundred percent of the students studied during the writing of this guide were awarded college scholarships. Surprisingly, 100% of those who received all-inclusive scholarships from major universities had also taken off-campus educational enrichment classes during their summer vacations and the weeks of Spring Break and Winter Break. None of the others had enrolled in such courses. Although all of the other recommendations in the *Free College* are helpful, this one may very well be the key to appearing more desirable to the individuals who head up college scholarship and grant programs.

The people who go through hundreds if not thousands of college applications each year look for students who are willing to go the extra mile in order to improve themselves.

Taking extra enrichment courses when not required to do so, certainly shows dedication. It makes applicants stand out from the crowd.

University personnel are also looking for some indication the individuals they select to receive scholarship or grant money will be successful once enrolled. Nothing is more frustrating to them than awarding hundreds of thousands of dollars to applicants who later flunk out or withdraw from school. By taking and passing enrichment courses, especially those offered by colleges or universities, young people show they can handle the rigor involved in college courses.

Enrichment classes can cover a wide variety of subjects. For example, Emma, who later won a comprehensive scholarship to the California Institute of Technology, took a summer course in electrical engineering and another in computer science at MIT. Not only did she learn a great deal, she enjoyed herself and came away with a letter of recommendation from each instructor. She used them later during her college application process.

Jacob, who later attended Duke University, studied Marine Biology at Hawaii Pacific University during the summer. Michael attended the Johns Hopkins Center for Talented Youth instead of taking a summer vacation trip with friends and ended up going to college there. Any enrichment classes high schoolers attend are best taken in subjects they enjoy and in which they have an aptitude. This is more likely to result in a positive experience and success. Also, they must not forget to collect letters of recommendation from each instructor at the end of the course.

In addition to enrichment classes, Full-Ride recipients often enrolled in required high school courses during summer school in order to make room in their regular session schedules for more advanced subjects. Earth Science, Study Skills, Biology, Keyboarding, Health and Web Design are examples of courses those in the study group were able to "get out of the way" during the shorter summer sessions.

It's easy to find required high school courses to take during the summer. Someone simply needs to look at the list of summer classes from the previous two years to see the pattern of offerings of the local high school. They can select courses in subjects that are fairly easy for the enrollee in order to have success in the limited time summer school provides. The student then enlists the help of a high school counselor so enrollment in the summer school class is assured.

Finding college enrichment courses isn't as simple. But by doing an online search of various university summer programs for high school students, a fairly comprehensive list can be created. It's also possible to go directly to the websites of specific universities to locate such programs. High school teachers are usually aware of university programs offered in their fields of expertise. They're a handy resource to tap into when looking for enrichment courses in specific subjects.

Aspirants need not limit themselves to the geographic area

where they live when selecting summer classes. Going far away from home in order to take advanced or university courses during summer vacation, shows college scholarship and grant committees the individual is self-sufficient and motivated. It also demonstrates the student's ability to stand on his or her own two feet.

The application process which results in free cash for college is a competition. Someone will win these grants and scholarships, but many others won't. In order to become the one who receives more free cash for college rather than less, it's necessary to get in the game. As German-born theoretical physicist Albert Einstein said, "You have to learn the rules of the game. And then you have to play better than anyone else."

## CHAPTER 2 - ACTION PLAN: (Parents until H.S., then Students)

Keep a running list of all enrichment classes taken by each of your children (separate page for each child, if possible); include date, name of course and instructor, and where class was taken.

_____
_____
_____
_____
_____
_____
_____
_____
_____
_____
_____
_____
_____
_____
_____
_____
_____
_____
_____
_____
_____

# FREE COLLEGE

Take Enrichment Classes

# FREE COLLEGE

# 3

## TAKE MUSIC LESSONS

*"Music is to the mind as air is to the body."*
*Plato*

Of the seventeen recommendations derived from the choices made by successful scholarship winners studied for the writing of this guide, this is the second most significant. **Over 75% of the Full-Ride Scholarship winners took private music lessons when they were young. The other 25% of these successful students took private lessons in the visual arts.** Only 8% of partial scholarship winners studied music or the visual arts outside of school hours.

People who study music early in life acquire better creative thinking and problem solving skills than those who haven't taken music lessons. These are traits that help high school graduates succeed in college and, therefore, make applicants more desirable. These candidates are often awarded more scholarship and grant money.

All of the grant and scholarship winners studied for this guide started taking music lessons or studying art beginning when they were young, often at around five years of age. They practiced from thirty to sixty minutes daily. They typically continued studying music or art until high school. One such individual, Olivia, who later attended MIT on a full scholarship, said she didn't especially enjoy studying the piano, but felt it really contributed to her mental development.

Another student who was awarded a substantial endowment which he applied to his studies at Northwestern University, Noah, studied both piano and violin while in elementary and middle school. He switched to playing the ukulele as a pastime while attending high school. It's typical of Full-Ride Scholarship winners to have studied several instruments (piano, violin, clarinet, guitar, etc.) while very young. They then turned to playing music recreationally during high school. A few played in their high school bands, but this was not the norm. Most reported discontinuing music study in high school, as practice no longer fit into their busy schedules.

None of those in the study group who took music lessons regretted doing so. This is true even of those whose parents initiated the lessons and selected the instrument. They all believed they derived a great deal of benefit from studying music. This is in line with studies which have been conducted on the effect of music education on learning.

The left portion of the brain, which controls language learning and reasoning, is more developed in people who have studied music. They also have more refined abilities in spatial relationships. This correlates to their development of better skills in both math and science. It also explains why music majors are admitted to medical schools at a higher rate than many other undergraduate majors.

Children who have been members of a musical group, orchestra or band received the added benefit of learning teamwork early in life. By performing in front of others, they gained self-confidence and developed the courage to take more risks. The ability to persist they acquired by practicing daily paid off whenever they came upon a difficult problem in academic subjects.

All of this is well-known in the offices of scholarship directors at colleges, universities and other groups which are responsible for selecting scholarship and grant winners. The National Educational Longitudinal Study reported high school students who have studied music have higher grade point averages than those who haven't. The College Entrance Examination Board has found applicants who have been enrolled in music appreciation classes scored sixty-three points higher on verbal examinations and forty-four points higher on math tests.

Since private music lessons and practice sessions take place after school hours, no school time is lost, but there are significant benefits. Performers often develop a love of music which they carry with them throughout their lives. This is demonstrated by how many go on to teach themselves to play additional instruments just for fun.

Those who studied the visual arts, dance or theater reaped similar benefits. They were more successful academically, had higher aspirations for their future careers and were more involved in civic activities than students who didn't participate in music or some other art forms.

It's most advantageous to have started studying music or the visual arts before or during elementary school. The enhanced brain development and skills acquired by doing so helped individuals become more successful academically throughout their school years. But it's never too late to add music or art lessons.

Studying music or art provided significant advantages for candidates when applying for grants and scholarships. Remember, all winners of substantial monetary awards had private lessons in music or the visual arts while growing up. Few of the others interviewed for this study had done so. It's a numbers game when seeking free cash to pay for college.

Studying music or the visual arts pays off in ways that may not be obvious, but are powerful nonetheless. President Bill Clinton once said to a reporter, "If I hadn't been exposed to music as a child, I don't think I would have been President."

## CHAPTER 3 - ACTION PLAN: (Parents)

Make a list of places where music, dance or art lessons can be found in your community; keep a record of which lessons are taken by each child by date, type of lesson, instructor and location.

_____
_____
_____
_____
_____
_____
_____
_____
_____
_____
_____
_____
_____
_____
_____
_____
_____
_____
_____
_____
_____
_____
_____
_____

Take Music Lessons

# FREE COLLEGE

# 4

## USE VISUAL AIDS

*"The key is not to prioritize what's on your schedule, but to schedule your priorities."*

*Steven Covey*

High school graduates who received Full-Ride Scholarships for college put this quote into practice. **Every one of them created visual aids in order to stay focused on doing the right thing at the right time.** Only 25% of students who received significantly less free money in college grants and scholarships followed this rule.

While many young people today use either paper plan books or electronic calendars to record their school assignments, **the most successful took this to the next level.** They made posters or kept a large white board in their bedrooms to remind themselves of what they needed to do. They kept this calendar visible at all times, so there was no possibility of forgetting either what must be completed or by when.

Another practical tactic used by many was to write new school assignments or upcoming responsibilities on sticky notes and place them in visible locations in their bedrooms as additional reminders. They were taken down and disposed of only after an assignment or task was completed. This is a similar process to that which has been used successfully in kitchens of busy restaurants for many years.

This prolific use of post-it notes is an effective way to call attention to the most important task at the moment or one which has an upcoming deadline. Susan, who received an extensive scholarship to USC, placed these notes not only in her daily planner and on her calendar, but on her bathroom mirror.

Color was frequently used to differentiate between subjects, assignments or events. Many did this by using colored markers or pens. This was especially typical of the most successful scholarship recipients. Eric, who received a large grant and went to the University of Michigan after graduation, used colored markers on the white board in his bedroom and in his weekly planner as well. Some high schoolers used colored three by five cards to create flashcards to remember upcoming events or due dates. They carried these with them at all times. They kept them most often in pencil pouches, wallets and backpacks.

No matter the specific manner scholarship winners transported information about their new assignments and tasks to their bedrooms, all of them had two things in common.

**First, they made sure they had some way to record important information with them at all times.** This could be anything from an expensive electronic device to something as old school as a tablet and pen.

**Second, 100% of Full-Ride students designated a location in their bedrooms where this information was on continuous display.** It was large, organized and updated often. They may have used different tools to record useful information initially, but their school assignments, meetings, practices and other tasks always ended up organized and presented in a prominent manner at home.

It was beneficial to have their current and upcoming assignments, tasks, appointments and responsibilities organized and on display. In addition to being a useful tool for time management, making this information visible means forgetting a task or missing a due date is less likely. According to Sara, who went to UC Santa Cruz and was one of the group who was able to attend college for free, this practice helped her be more successful in her studies.

But there is another benefit to using a large poster or white board in this way. Those who do so have less anxiety and are less stressed out. They're confident that they aren't likely to forget something. Their fear of failure is reduced, allowing them to be more self-confident. They can manage their workload because they're able to see what they need to do and by when it needs to be done.

According to Johns Hopkins School of Education, it's the individual's perception of events (work) that determines his response (success). They learn best when in a calm and relaxed state. When they feel a situation is out of their control, they aren't as able to access the higher order thinking centers of their brains. By having their work organized and visible, individuals are able to size up their situations and better cope with the amount of work they must complete in a fixed amount of time.

This organizational tool provides encouragement and positive motivation for those who use it. According to neurologist J. Willis MD, "Positive motivation impacts brain metabolism." As students become more emotionally resilient, they learn more efficiently. They also learn at higher levels.

Stress interferes with memory. By using a memory aid that is visible at all times, an individual's level of stress is reduced. The more organized he becomes, the more he is relaxed and calm enough to complete required assignments.

People who use this method to organize themselves are taking maximum advantage of Stephen Covey's third habit from his book, *Seven Habits of Highly Effective People*. They're better able to "Put First Things First." Although many in high school are wedded to their smartphones and tablets, those who also used non-electronic reminders received far more money in scholarships and grants.

A large poster or white board placed on continuous display

in a visible location in a candidate's bedroom is a useful tool in the quest to receive more free cash for college. It may not seem significant to the casual observer, but **students who have received the most money in grants and scholarships used some form of this mechanism to stay organized.** As John Heywood, English writer, musician and composer, correctly warned us back in the 1500s, "Out of sight, out of mind."

## CHAPTER 4 - ACTION PLAN: (Parents until H.S, then Students)

Create and record a schedule for checking day planners and wall calendars of each child.

# Use Visual Aids

## FREE COLLEGE

## Use Visual Aids

# FREE COLLEGE

# 5

## EAT BREAKFAST DAILY

*"One should not attend even the end of the world without a good breakfast."*

Robert A. Heinlein

One hundred percent of Full-Ride recipients ate a healthy breakfast daily. Hundreds of studies have been completed with volumes of evidence proving eating a nutritious breakfast daily has a positive effect on learning. Student behavior, cognitive function and academic performance are enhanced for those who eat breakfast regularly. They're more awake and alert and are better able to pay attention in class. They also remember more information than those who come to school with an empty stomach.

Eating a healthy breakfast and getting a good night's sleep are basic requirements for success in school. Despite this fact, only 25% of the applicants who received partial scholarships reported eating breakfast regularly. This was a mistake they later regretted.

**Many Full-Ride recipients planned their breakfast the night before.** This is an efficient habit which makes time between getting up and arrival at school less stressful. Their breakfasts usually contained whole grain, whole wheat bread or crackers, eggs, tuna or chicken, milk and/or cheese and fruit.

**Others preferred getting up earlier to prepare and eat breakfast before leaving for school.** Sometimes they did this on their own. On other occasions, they assisted a parent in making the meal. If they were running late, the food was packed and consumed in the car on the way to school while a parent drove.

Emily, a recipient of an all-inclusive college scholarship to Claremont College, explained her mother insisted upon getting up before the children in the family each morning. She prepared a healthy breakfast for them daily. Both parents required Emily and her siblings to finish breakfast before leaving for school. Emily reported she was grateful for this family tradition.

A few mentioned they had trouble digesting large meals in the morning. This didn't mean they skipped breakfast, however. They just ate something lighter like fruit and/or a hard-boiled egg. **In every case, the students who ate breakfast regularly did better in school and received more scholarship money.**

In order to reap the most benefits, a well-balanced breakfast was eaten each morning. Wholegrain bread, toast or muffins provided necessary nutrients. Nuts, nut butters, eggs, beans, tuna or chicken added protein which the brain needs to function. Cereals they selected were made from whole grains (like oatmeal) and there was no added sugar. Fresh fruit the students preferred was included.

If processed foods were selected, then the labels showing both ingredients and nutritional information were examined. **Shortcuts are fine, as long as the food selected is healthy and includes complex carbohydrates, protein and fiber, but doesn't include added sugars.** When added sugars are consumed, there is an inevitable crash and burn short-circuiting learning.

Employees of institutions awarding grants and scholarships didn't ask about eating habits, and yet every Full-Ride Scholarship recipient started his/her morning with a healthy breakfast. While there might not be a direct cause and effect link between eating breakfast daily and receiving scholarship and grant money, the relationship between the two is too obvious to ignore.

It may take effort to organize a healthy breakfast each morning and to take the time to consume it, but the benefits are profound. This is an investment in a child's health, education and future. As one of our Founding Fathers Benjamin Franklin said, "An investment in knowledge pays the best interest."

## CHAPTER 5 - ACTION PLAN: (Parents)

Divide these lined pages into quarters (using a colored marker); create a breakfast menu in each section; use them to help in making shopping lists and creating a breakfast routine.

# 6

## START LOOKING EARLY

*"Opportunities are like sunrises.*
*If you wait too long, you miss them."*
William Arthur Ward

According to the Department of Education, over $46 billion are available to high school graduates each year in the form of college scholarships. Then why do over 60% of college graduates have student loan debt? **Perhaps they waited too long to start looking for help paying for their education.**

Mia had her pick of the best scholarships. She was wooed by MIT, Harvard and Yale. I asked her when she had started looking into colleges. This is what she told me. "Since my freshman year, I have been looking at different colleges I'm interested in attending. This way, I've had something to work towards and a plan for my future. I looked at scholarships they might offer at the same time."

She had this in common with other successful scholarship applicants. **100% of Full-Ride Scholarship winners started exploring options for college in their freshman year or earlier.** Only 20% of those awarded less scholarship money began looking into colleges that early.

Ethan, who earned far less money, which he applied to his tuition at Cal State University, Fullerton, explained. "At the start of my senior year, I began to look for scholarships to pay for college." He had far less time than Mia to investigate, make his choices and apply for scholarships. He earned only a fraction of the amount many others earned, despite being equally talented and having similar grades and SAT scores.

Procrastination can be expensive. It can cost as much as a college education. It has been detrimental to many who needed financial aid for college. As Benjamin Franklin said, "You may delay, but time will not." We all know time is money. While some are going to the movies, others are communicating with colleges and getting a leg up on the competition.

Opportunity cost is a term used in economics. This is the loss of potential gain (like scholarship money) from other alternatives (doing research) when one alternative (socializing or playing video games) is selected. It explains why some deserving scholars miss out. Putting aside a few hours each week to research colleges and possible sources of scholarship money means something must be sacrificed. It's the trade-off that pays off.

Start Looking Early

Some high schoolers did their research on their own using their personal computers. Others worked in pairs or small groups and shared information. A few stayed after school from time to time and used the school career or college center. Some worked on computers in the school library. It really didn't matter where the work took place.

All of the individuals in the study signed up on http://www.fastweb.com. This is an online tool for researching scholarships for college. Another online resource is http://scholly.com. This site matches graduates with grants as well as with scholarships. But applicants need to contact colleges and universities directly as well. Online tools make general information available, but usually don't provide specifics on facilities and programs at individual universities.

There are two separate tasks which need to be completed. Individuals need to first narrow down the field they're interested in pursuing as a future career (math, music, art, engineering, etc.). Once their choice is made, they identify accredited colleges offering a complete program in that specific field. Those colleges which don't help prepare for his or her chosen future profession can be eliminated, saving a vast amount of time and effort.

In addition to websites, there are two books which will help with this research. One is *Confessions of a Scholarship Winner* by Kristina Ellis. The author's parents couldn't help her pay for college. She needed scholarships and/or grants to do so. Her book tells the steps she took to pay for college. Her story begins at the start of high school. The steps she took worked for her, but it's easier to prepare earlier. Still, her book is a useful source of information.

Another detailed how-to type book is *Free $ for College for Dummies* by David Rosen and Caryn Mladen. This book contains detailed information about the nuts and bolts of applying for scholarships and grants. It does a good job at this, but doesn't cover the critical issue of how to differentiate oneself from another applicant. It's an excellent reference guide for those who don't have access to a high school counselor who specializes in college admissions and scholarships.

High school students who start looking into colleges and seeking scholarships early enjoy their senior year far more than those who have put this off until the last minute. They're less stressed, therefore, able to handle their college visits and interviews far better. Making a good impression increases the odds an applicant will be successful in being awarded a Full-Ride Scholarship.

I had the opportunity to observe hundreds of pupils from their freshman year through graduation four years later. I was able to see the self-confidence and relaxed nature of those who didn't procrastinate. I also witnessed the frantic efforts and fear in those who had put things off to the last minute. As President Abraham Lincoln stated, "Things may come to those who wait, but only the things left by those who hustle."

# CHAPTER 6 - ACTION PLAN: (Parents and Students together)

Create a weekly schedule for researching appropriate colleges and scholarships for each child; record them here.

_____
_____
_____
_____
_____
_____
_____
_____
_____
_____
_____
_____
_____
_____
_____
_____
_____
_____
_____
_____
_____
_____
_____
_____

# FREE COLLEGE

# 7

## GET NOTICED

*"Nothing brings about success like walking through the right doors."*

Steven Berglas

The high school college counselor is an expert at knowing which doors to open. **100% of Full-Ride Scholarship winners bonded with their counselors early in high school.** Isabella, who later attended Barnard College on a substantial scholarship, explained what she did in her freshman year. "At first I thought being a squeaky wheel would be bad because I would annoy my counselor. I didn't want to make a bad first impression. But I noticed getting to know my counselor in a good way, by asking questions, made it easy for her to learn my name. I thought this could help me in high school, which it has tremendously. Now, I'm not scared to ask questions."

It's best not to wait until late in high school to become friends with this very important person on campus. The counselor should already know the student's name and post high school goals long before he reaches his senior year. This is crucial as the typical American high school has an enrollment of well over 800, and many have far more. A single person can get lost in the crowd unless she does something to call attention to herself in a positive way.

Asking questions is always a good way to get noticed. Most don't do this, so someone who does stands out for all the right reasons. It shows an interest in the subject the counselor is explaining. It also prevents making critical mistakes, which is imperative when applying for college admission and scholarships. Counselors are often asked to write letters of recommendation. It's much easier for them to write effective letters when they have known the subject of the letter for several years.

Madison, who went to Syracuse University after graduation, told me staying close to Mrs. Evans, her counselor, definitely helped with college applications. She learned about requirements, recommendations and deadlines long before they came along. This helped her avoid mistakes when deciding which classes to take, extra-curricular activities to choose or service organizations to join. It's better to have someone looking out for you, than being on your own.

None of the seniors who reported bonding with their counselors early had anything negative to say about the experience. Their classmates didn't taunt them for doing so. Mostly, they didn't even notice, but the counselors did. Often school office personnel learn the names of individuals with problems long before those of students who are college bound. So becoming a good-natured "squeaky wheel" adds a bit of positivity to a counselor's day. Those who greet their counselor when passing in the hall reinforce the constructive relationship their previous interactions began.

Daniel, a scholarship winner to the University Of Notre Dame, said he "hung around" his counselor because she was a "cool lady who was easy to talk to and knew a lot about college." As future graduates accumulate knowledge of college requirements their self-confidence increases. This makes them more optimistic and upbeat in class.

Those for whom college remains a mystery are less likely to take the correct high school courses, participate in extra-curricular activities or join service organizations. All of these are necessary if someone is aiming for college admission, scholarships or grants. Charlotte, who later went to UCLA with a sizable scholarship, explained her counselor, Mr. Johnson, helped her often and always had an answer for her questions. She said she spoke up in order to get the attention she needed. She was effective in her efforts and wasn't only accepted by the college of her choice, but awarded an impressive scholarship.

All who earned substantial scholarships or grants learned the names of their high school college counselor during their freshman year. They developed a positive relationship with this individual and made sure he/she also knew who they were. **Only 15% of students who were awarded smaller amounts of scholarship money took the time to become acquainted with their college counselor.**

High school counselors have the responsibility to make sure each college bound person in the school is enrolled in the correct courses and fulfills all other requirements for college admission. They're also the "go to" person for college scholarships, grants and loans. Often this job rests on the shoulders of one individual on campus. It's an overwhelming task.

Each student must take the first step in making sure his needs are met. Bonding with the college counselor will put the college hopeful in an advantageous position. The best time to learn the name of the advisor is when a ninth grader takes his introductory tour of the high school campus as an incoming freshman. **He can then introduce himself to this essential member of the school faculty during the first two weeks of school.** Putting it off is risky. As Hungarian composer Franz Liszt warned, "Beware of missing chances; otherwise it may be altogether too late one day."

## CHAPTER 7 - ACTION PLAN: (Students)

Find out the name of your counselor; ascertain the campus "expert" on all things college; visit both regularly to learn the steps necessary for applying for college, scholarships and grants; record them here.

_____
_____
_____
_____
_____
_____
_____
_____
_____
_____
_____
_____
_____
_____
_____
_____
_____
_____
_____
_____
_____
_____
_____
_____

# FREE COLLEGE

# 8

## JOIN STUDY GROUPS

*"Many hands make light work."*
*John Heywood*

Although the size of the groups varied, 100% of Full-Ride Scholarship winners met with other students to study. Only 20% of students who received less money made use of study groups. Not all high school students join study groups. Many choose to study alone. But those who find a friend or group of friends with whom to study soon discover the work is easier. They also realized they learn more than when they go it alone.

Ava, one of those who earned several scholarships, was accepted where she wanted to go to college, Vanderbilt University. She said she thought study groups were useless at first; they were made up of strangers who met in the library for help. But she found by "hanging out" with friends a study group formed naturally.

She and her friends created informal seminars related to subjects they were studying and projects they were assigned. She was pleasantly surprised to find she had fun learning this way. It was easier to get started on a difficult project because she wasn't alone. As American writer Margaret Carty explained, "The nice thing about teamwork is that you always have others on your side."

Liam joined study groups because he realized he would be able to absorb information from different members in the groups. He liked being able to see more than one point of view or perspective on a particular subject when working with others. As with most who participate in study groups, he improved his performance on tests and projects. He met with others before exams or just before a project was due. If he wasn't meeting with one of his groups, he maintained contact by telephone. He won a large scholarship and attended the University of Pennsylvania upon graduation.

Students planned their study sessions in advance. They kept each other on track and worked diligently together, according to Abigail, who received a complete scholarship to the University of Riverside at graduation. Some groups met during the week, others on the weekend. Most met for special study sessions the day before a test was scheduled.

Study partners work the same way as study groups. Sam and Katie met in their math class in seventh grade. They began studying together soon thereafter. They realized they had several other subjects in common and increased their study time to include these subjects. They continued this relationship throughout secondary school. They planned their school schedules to have classes in common whenever possible.

Their friendship didn't end when they graduated and attended universities on separate coasts. Their get-togethers changed from in person to over the Internet. Katie graduated from NYU this June and Sam from Pomona College one week later. Both were debt-free.

Studies have shown individuals who make use of informal study groups have a more positive attitude towards their work. Stress, tension and anxiety are reduced. Their self-esteem and confidence is often higher than in those who study alone. There is also an added benefit to people making use of such groups. They build better communication skills. This not only helps them in high school, but also when applying for college admission, scholarships and grants.

Margaret Mead, American cultural anthropologist, wasn't referring to high school or college scholarships when she said, "Never doubt that a small group of thoughtful, committed people can change the world." But her comment can be applied to high school students seeking scholarships. **A small group of dedicated students can help each other improve their chances of receiving a Full-Ride Scholarship for college.** It happens all the time.

## CHAPTER 8 - ACTION PLAN: (Students)

Determine in which classes you would benefit from having a study partner or study group; find friends to join, create a schedule and find a location; record information here.

_____
_____
_____
_____
_____
_____
_____
_____
_____
_____
_____
_____
_____
_____
_____
_____
_____
_____
_____
_____
_____
_____
_____
_____
_____

# Join Study Groups

# FREE COLLEGE

# Join Study Groups

## 9

## FOCUS

*"When you focus on what you want,
everything else falls away."*
Rhonda Byrne

Full-Ride Scholarship recipients have learned focus sets their direction and brings meaning to everything they do. They have become experts at making simple everyday choices based upon their ultimate goal. This gives them a grounded purpose and a sense of calm.

Their short term goals are based upon their long term desires. They are, therefore, not easily distracted. When studying or completing a project, they don't allow their electronics or other outside interruptions to take them off course. The simple way they accomplish this is by turning off their electronic devices, music, television and shutting the door to the room in which they're working. They take control and don't waste time.

By avoiding distractions, they're able to make better decisions. They're able to concentrate on what needs to be completed at any one moment. Any resistance they meet from friends or family members doesn't sidetrack them for very long. They're able to stay on task and get things done.

They don't multi-task or shift their attention, as to do either invites failure. They find it's better to do one thing at a time, and to do it well rather than attempting to complete several tasks simultaneously. This only results in poor quality work. **Successful scholarship recipients are persistent and dedicated about their work and their goals.** Kevin, who earned a very large college scholarship to Cal State University, Long Beach, said he "just targeted one thing at a time and did what had to be done." It's like adjusting a camera lens so one object is in sharp focus, the rest (the distractions) blur into the background.

Visual, written and mental reminders of their objective took several forms. Some students had college pennants hanging in their rooms. Others put up posters of the colleges they wished to attend. A few made vision books and looked at them before bed each night. At the end of the day, when they assessed their daily activities to make sure what they did was in alignment with their goals, they were able to see their objective right in front of them. This has a profound impact.

**Successful graduates learned to keep their eye on the prize. In this way, they were able to conquer their fear.** Alex, who received a sizeable college award, several grants and attended

Loyola Marymount University after graduation, explained he didn't need to be obsessive or stressed out. He didn't overwork himself. He just made sure to do everything that needed to be done without worrying about being perfect. Steve Jobs, technology entrepreneur and inventor, said "The two enemies of focus are distraction and fear." Full-Ride students conquer both.

Single-mindedness enhances productivity. Without it, a person's abilities suffer. When a workspace is decluttered and simple, it's easier to perform at a consistently higher level. Those who organized and decluttered their work space were more effective and efficient. This is in line with the comments of Dr. Jim Taylor, Ph.D., professor and author. He said people would produce, "better quality work, more success and achievement of goals" when attention is controlled.

Secondary school is a journey. By targeting the ultimate goal and not allowing anxiety or distractions to interfere with doing what is necessary, an all-inclusive college scholarship is within reach. As Brian Tracy, author and motivational speaker, explained, "The key to success is to focus our conscious mind on things we desire, not things we fear."

## CHAPTER 9 - ACTION PLAN: (Students)

Record short term and long term goals here; display visual reminders in your bedroom; declutter work space regularly.

# FREE COLLEGE

Focus

# FREE COLLEGE

## 10

## COMPLETE EVERY ASSIGNMENT

*"Great ability develops and reveals itself increasingly with every new assignment."*
Baltasar Gracian

Full-Ride Scholarship winners know there are many benefits obtained by completing each and every school assignment. One important factor is mathematical. Everyone knows a high grade point average is crucial in landing scholarships and grants. The GPA is made up of the final grades earned in high school classes. But not everyone completely understands the devastation failure to turn in an assignment has on the final semester grade.

Most teachers employ the 90/80/70 method in computing grades. An "A" grade is assigned to those who have 90% or more of their answers correct. A "B" goes to those with 80% to 89% correct and so on. Students don't often realize a failing grade still earns points. They can actually earn up to fifty points when failing a test or assignment.

**Failure to complete an assignment, however, means many points are being left on the table.** At the end of each grading period, when grades are computed, that zero will yield a dreadful result. A simple way to illustrate this is by comparing two imaginary students. Jimmy completes both projects which were assigned. He earns a perfect score of 100 points out of 100 possible on the first one. That is an "A". He earns only 50 points of 100 possible on the other, which is an "F". His final grade in the course averages 75%, which is a "C".

Johnny, however, completes only one assignment. He has a perfect score and earns 100 points of 100 possible, but he receives nothing on the assignment he didn't complete. When the scores are totaled, his final grade is only 50%, which is an "F" in the course. Looking at the entire number of assignments in a class and assuming doing most of the work is good enough if those assignments earned high marks, is a mistake. The example above, on the other hand, illustrates this is mathematically impossible. **Students can't dig themselves out of the hole failure to turn in all assignments creates.**

Another advantage of completing everything comes from what is learned in the trying. As Neil Gaiman, novelist and screenwriter, said, "Whatever it takes to finish things, finish. You'll learn more from a glorious failure than you ever will from something you never finished." Mary, who earned a sizable college scholarship to Whittier College, had a simple goal for herself. She wanted to complete every assignment she was given in four years of high school, and she did.

Kevin also earned a Full-Ride Scholarship. He taught himself time management by reading Sean Covey's *Seven Habits of Successful Teens*, so he could finish all of the work and turn it in when it was due. He did his homework each night, and started major projects well in advance. He used the weekends to study for upcoming exams. He took these habits with him when he attended the Fashion Institute of Design and Merchandising in San Francisco where he was very successful.

**Self-confidence and lower levels of stress and anxiety come when work is completed.** Entering a classroom without a finished project on the day it's due creates fear. No one is happy when a name is called, and someone has to say, "I don't have it." Nick also experienced distress at home when he skipped an assignment. He didn't want to disappoint his parents, so he finished them all. While this isn't the best kind of motivation, it served him well in the end, as he earned good grades and a large college scholarship to Cornell.

Teachers put a great deal of time and expertise into the design of their lesson plans. Each task has an educationally sound basis. Although it's best if students understand the reasons behind each lesson and assignment, it isn't really necessary. It's enough to know those who do, get, and those who don't do, don't get. They don't earn good grades, and they don't receive major college scholarships either.

Helen Keller, author, political activist and lecturer, put it well when she explained, "I long to accomplish a great and noble task, but it is my chief duty to accomplish small tasks as if they were great and noble."

# CHAPTER 10 - ACTION PLAN: (Parents and Students)

Create daily or weekly schedule for checking homework and long term projects; record schedule here.

_____
_____
_____
_____
_____
_____
_____
_____
_____
_____
_____
_____
_____
_____
_____
_____
_____
_____
_____
_____
_____
_____
_____

# FREE COLLEGE

## Complete Every Assignment

# FREE COLLEGE

## 11

## ASK QUESTIONS

*"People who don't ask questions remain clueless throughout their lives."*

*Neil deGrasse Tyson*

William, who was awarded a Full-Ride Scholarship to USC, put it quite simply. **"When I needed help, I asked for help."** He gave the example of not understanding how to complete a difficult math assignment. He just asked the teacher. He explained, "She won't bite." This is a classic example of the acronym for the word FEAR, false expectations appearing real. Most people who don't ask questions hold back out of some sort of fear. Perhaps they don't want to appear foolish. In reality, however, remaining ignorant when help is available is the epitome of foolishness.

**The impatience of Full-Ride students to reach their goals eliminates fear.** They tolerate momentarily discomfort in order to obtain clarity. They keep their eye on the prize and don't let outward appearances get in the way. **Future scholarship winners know their true friends will not make fun of them for asking questions, and the opinion of others doesn't matter.**

There are several different places for students to get help when they're stuck or confused. James, who received a large scholarship to attend Cal Poly Pomona, said the first thing he did when he didn't know what was going on was to ask his friends. If he still didn't understand after obtaining their help, he went to the teacher for assistance, but he didn't stop there. If the teacher's explanation didn't clear things up for him, he asked the teacher to explain it another way. That usually did the trick.

Others reversed the procedure. They often asked the teacher on the spot. They weren't reluctant to raise their hands during class instruction. This shortened the length of time in which they remained confused, which allowed them to retain more information from the rest of the lesson.

There's an additional benefit to asking questions during class time. It often helps classmates, especially those who are too afraid to ask questions. This develops a sense of camaraderie which improves the learning environment for all.

There's a useful method to improve success when working a math problem or performing a similar task. Asking a peer who has a better grasp of the materials to sit and watch when a problem is being worked out is invaluable. By observing as each step is performed, the friend can spot where the thought process goes off track and suggest the correct operation.

**The most important reasons to ask questions in school are to obtain information and to achieve clarity.** But there are other benefits as well. People who ask questions are often thought of as more intelligent. It gives an indication someone is thinking, cares about the subject at hand and wants to learn. These are always good perceptions.

It also makes the person being asked for assistance feel more important. When advice or help is sought, the recipient of the request usually feels respected and important. These are additional good impressions to leave with someone in a position of authority. It shows character when an individual is willing to put himself out there by asking questions. Peter Drucker, management consultant, educator and author, once said his greatest strength was "to be ignorant and ask a few questions."

## CHAPTER 11 - ACTION PLAN: (Students)

Develop a routine for asking questions in difficult classes; raise your hand and ask the teacher; ask a friend after class; ask the teacher after class; work with study group; if still confused, find a tutor; record names of mentors and scheduled meetings here.

_____

_____

_____

_____

_____

_____

_____

_____

_____

_____

_____

_____

_____

_____

_____

_____

_____

_____

_____

_____

# FREE COLLEGE

# Ask Questions

# FREE COLLEGE

## 12

## BEFRIEND COMPETITIVE PEOPLE

*"The better you are at surrounding yourself with people of high potential, the greater your chance of success."*
John Maxwell

Full-Ride Scholarship winners have improved upon John Maxwell's quote. **They surround themselves with high achieving competitive people of high potential.** By doing so, they're always motivated to do well. Peer pressure can be either a good thing or bad. By using it to encourage themselves to work hard and achieve more, these students are using human nature to their advantage.

Parents are rightly concerned about the friends their children make. People become like those with whom they associate. Individuals can decide to befriend someone who is high or low achieving. They can talk about sports or the next exam. They can follow the latest pop star on Facebook or their favorite university. Choices matter. Making them consciously, with future goals in mind can have a profound effect upon how much scholarship money is received and upon overall success.

Julia, who received a large scholarship to attend UC Berkeley, said she thought it was a good idea to have really smart people as friends. She said **she learned new things all the time and was always challenged when she was around competitive people.** This prepared her well for the competition she would encounter later in college.

While moving through high school, teenagers form bonds with each other. When they choose friends well, what they learn from each other will give them an advantage over those who chose less wisely. People share experiences and ideas. They work together and play together. It's the mix of the two that's different when associated with competitive people. They do have fun, but fun just might be getting a high mark on a project for school.

**It's far easier to remain motivated and productive when those around you have similar goals.** It may sound cold, but hanging out with those who don't share the desire to achieve will make it more difficult to do so. Gabriela earned enough scholarship money to cover four years at the college of her choice. She said her competitive friends always helped her strive to achieve higher grades.

The greatest race ever run (1989) took place between two competitive Iron Man athletes. During this event, two athletes swam, ran and biked neck and neck. They pushed each other. Research has shown when people perform in groups; their results are far greater than when they work alone. In this case the competition was athletic, but it also holds true for academics. A competitive setting has a major beneficial effect upon performance.

As Matt Fitzgerald, writer, trainer and competitive runner, suggests to athletes in his article, "Does Competition Improve Performance?", students would be well served by finding, "a group that's bound to have at least one member who's a step faster (better) and can pull (them) along to a new level of performance."

## CHAPTER 12 - ACTION PLAN: (Students)

Record names of competitive people in each school subject; ask if any would like to be your study partner or join your study group.

…

## 13

## COMMIT TO EXTRACURRICULAR ACTIVITIES

*"We are what we repeatedly do."*
*Aristotle*

In addition to studying music, as covered in a previous chapter of this book, **100 % of Full-Ride scholarship winners threw themselves into a variety of extracurricular activities.** They did this for different reasons, but they all reported being keenly aware colleges judge students' character by what they do in their after school hours. Each one of them participated in several after school programs throughout their four years of high school.

They played a variety of sports, mostly those which included being on a team such as tennis or basketball. Carlos, who received enough scholarship money to cover college tuition, was on his school badminton team. He said he became more disciplined and learned how to be a leader while doing so. Walter Annenberg, American publisher, philanthropist and diplomat, said playing on a team provides "training that will prove invaluable later on in life."

Sports and other physical activities build stamina and strengthen the immune system. In addition to these two health benefits, they create an environment which relieves anxiety. The relaxation they foster helps avoid depression. **Colleges are on the lookout for activities that might help students avoid burn-out.**

Another team building activity which takes place both during and after school hours is ASB (Associated Student Body) or Student Council as it's called in some school districts. It's the governing body which organizes social activities and runs everything from school dances to charity events. It's considered a service group, although members usually earn credits towards graduation for participation.

Several graduates who earned comprehensive scholarships, as well as others who received less scholarship or grant money, served as members of such organizations. There they learned time management and leadership skills, as well as how to set priorities. They also became better at dealing with people who were different from themselves or who had dissimilar interests. Students who remained involved throughout three or four years of high school refined their social skills well beyond those who didn't.

Involvement in school related extracurricular activities, clubs, sports, theater, ASB, honorary societies, music groups, etc.

requires a higher grade point average be maintained. This is added motivation for some. These groups often provide additional academic help for those who need it.

Community service groups not affiliated with the school system were also targeted by successful scholarship winners. Some students found service organizations (like the Lions Club) or opportunities to volunteer (church youth groups) through their parents. Others were discovered while investigating future career plans (helping out at veterinary clinics). **Giving to others helps build a résumé and higher self-esteem as well.**

College admission personnel like seeing a history of community service, varied interests, an adventurous nature and sustained commitment when looking through the history of extracurricular activities of an applicant. They infer the character of the individual from his choices. As John Maxwell wrote, "People who use time wisely spend it on activities that advance their overall purpose in life."

## CHAPTER 13 - ACTION PLAN: (Parents until H.S., then Students)

List "on campus" and "off campus" extracurricular activities of each child; date, activity, coach/advisor/leader, location.

## Commit to Extracurricular Activities

## Commit to Extracurricular Activities

## 14

## DINE AS A FAMILY

*"Sharing a family meal is good for the spirit, the brain and the health of all family members."*
*Anne Fishel*

Dining together as a family at least five days each week was reported by 100% of Full-Ride Scholarship winners studied for this book. Eighty percent of all other scholarship winners in the group did so as well. On the other hand, one in four students in the U.S. doesn't eat with their parents even two nights each week. Mealtime may seem insignificant, but all studies on the topic show this is a key factor leading to student success.

Frequently sharing meals creates healthy relationships between parent and child. Angie, who earned an enviable college scholarship to Stanford, said eating dinner with her family was the way she was raised, and it felt "weird" when they didn't eat together. Angie was brimming with self-confidence, happy and well-adjusted. She, like other students, explained her family chatted and shared small talk while dining.

This wasn't a time for discussion of family conflicts or chores. The children weren't grilled about homework or school projects during these meals. Instead, they conversed about daily events, items in the news, future plans, and gossip about celebrities. They even told stories. **It was the act of chatting together that built family fellowship and a sense of belonging.**

The National Center on Addiction and Substance Abuse at Columbia University found there are many benefits of sharing family meals at least five times each week. There were lower rates of substance and alcohol abuse, teenaged pregnancies and eating disorders. Vocabularies were improved. GPAs were higher, as was self-esteem. Family meals build resilience into children's personalities. They're better adjusted in social environments because of the attention and validation they received.

By making an effort to spend time together eating and talking on a regular basis, youngsters feel they matter to their parents and to other members of their families. They realize they're both visible and important. They learn they can count on their parents to "be there" for them.

Although it may be difficult or inconvenient to organize family meals so often, as author Steven Covey wrote, "The main thing is to keep the main thing the main thing." **Families who make a shared dinner time a priority raise happier**

Dine as a Family

and more successful children than those who do not. If this is an essential goal, and if college loan debt is to be avoided, then finding a way to make this happen is prudent.

It doesn't matter where these meals take place, but they need to be in environments that are conducive to talking. Eating in front of the television doesn't provide the same benefits. Telephones and other electronics should be turned off during the meal. Children can help with meal planning, aid in meal preparation, set the table or not. The family could dine in a restaurant, neighborhood café or at the kitchen table.

Meals don't need to be as elaborate or families as large as they are depicted at Sunday dinners on television shows. But the rest of what happens there is the goal. The family chats. They discuss work, school, current events and anything else which comes to mind.

Logan, who went to UC Davis on a full scholarship after graduation, described his family's evening meal. **He said they all shared what their day was like.** He said his family helped him talk through difficult decisions about school and in his life. He felt supported by his family. This paid off in many ways, especially when he earned his college scholarship.

The differences between children whose families hold discussions at mealtimes and those who don't are apparent. High school senior Susan listened to a classroom conversation about the benefits of dining together as a family, and her eyes filled with tears. She confided her parents never ate dinner with her. They spent their time taking her brother to various sporting activities and left her alone to fend for herself. She had problems with self-esteem and often didn't have the courage to participate in oral debates in class. She was bright and earned some scholarship money, but not nearly as much as others, who were less gifted, but felt more validated by family.

If receiving a large amount of college scholarship money is appealing, then rearranging schedules so the family can dine together at least five days each week should be a priority. As successful American businessman and humorist Arnold H. Glasow explained, in order to be successful, one must, "do what's right, the right way, at the right time."

# CHAPTER 14 - ACTION PLAN: (Parents and Students)

Record the work/school/activity schedule for the entire family on one large calendar; display evening activities; schedule family dinners a minimum of five nights each week; set "rules" (electronic free zone); update as needed.

Dine as a Family

## 15

## FIND A MENTOR

*"Mentors know what it takes to succeed."*
*Steven Berglas*

Every Full-Ride Scholarship recipient found a mentor while in high school. So did 60% of the other scholarship and grant winners reviewed for this book. They didn't use the term "mentor", however, but referred to them as "people who are older and on the path you want to follow." These mentors provided both guidance and encouragement. Students gained information, self-confidence and a network of advisors. Some of them were family members, others weren't.

Amy, who earned a large college scholarship and later attended Biola University, said this was easy to accomplish because she had two older sisters who looked after her. Their friends also came to her aid when she needed advice about which classes to take, how to deal with the workload or other school related problems. She was especially grateful they shared their past mistakes with her so she could avoid making them.

Nicholas was advised by his cousin who was three years ahead of him in school. He gives his cousin credit for convincing him to participate in the International Baccalaureate Program. This program not only challenged him to develop strong academic habits, but led him to a Full-Ride Scholarship at Dartmouth University.

Edwin said it was easy to find someone to emulate because his older brother was enrolled at the University of Riverside, his college goal. When he needed help, he asked. Since the college was fairly close, he was able to reach his brother whenever necessary. Edwin received a scholarship, and followed his brother to the University of Riverside.

Not all children belong to families which provide students with older siblings or cousins who can mentor them. When this is the case, **older friends can fulfill the role.** Matt said he had several older friends who explained to him how they reached college. He followed their examples and went to Pomona College with a substantial scholarship.

Annie was an only child and preferred to ask adults for mentoring, rather than older students. She didn't hesitate to ask questions because she thought it was smart to ask an individual who had more experience and wisdom. **She was never embarrassed to ask questions when she didn't know what to**

**do.** Those who helped her, (her coach, pastor, neighbor, etc.) were happy to do so. It's flattering to be asked for advice by an intelligent child who is looking to get ahead, and she did. Annie was awarded a substantial scholarship to Princeton University.

Vivian, a successful scholarship winner who enrolled at UC Irvine, asked adults, but her reasons were far different than those of others. She didn't trust her own generation, thinking most too young and not serious about getting ahead. Therefore, she sought guidance from older people. She liked their attitude better and was able to seek advice from those who had already become successful.

Celine chose to befriend people who already had the career she wanted. She found mentors by going to conferences, workshops and conventions. She did what most people won't. She asked for help. This way, she learned from those who were firmly established where she wanted to go. Celine was able to gain a large amount of firsthand knowledge and was certain the advice she received was accurate. It became obvious this was, in fact, the career path she wanted to follow from discussions with these mentors. She knew which classes to take and which enrichment programs to attend. A generous scholarship was the result, and Georgetown University became her college destination.

Having a mentor supply advice, information and encouragement is so essential, one is provided to each Bill and Melinda Gates Millennium Scholarship winner. **Students need not**

**wait until after high school graduation to acquire a mentor, however.** They should be like President Woodrow Wilson who said, "I not only use all the brains I have, but all I can borrow."

## CHAPTER 15 - ACTION PLAN: (Students)

Find an older sibling, cousin, friend or adult (coach, pastor, friend of family) or instructor (met at a conference, enrichment course, etc.) to act as your mentor; record schedule of meetings and advice here.

# FREE COLLEGE

## Find a Mentor

# FREE COLLEGE

## 16

## MAKE WISE CHOICES

*Success is nothing more than a few simple disciplines,
practiced every day.*
Jim Rohn

Every student interviewed for this book thought making wise choices was crucial to success in high school and being accepted into college. They believed **when making a decision, the option that should be selected is the one which brings you closer to reaching your goal.** By doing so, not only are success in high school and acceptance into college achieved, but scholarships are earned.

In order to make appropriate choices, it's important to focus on the desired outcome. Those looking to earn an all-inclusive scholarship should do as Steven Covey stated, **"begin with the end in mind."** It may seem more logical to concentrate on the options themselves, but this allows distractions to creep into the equation. When the final objective is firmly established, the wheat is separated from the chaff. This eliminates alternatives that aren't necessary to accomplish the task. It also creates clarity and simplifies the decision making process.

As Jessica, who earned a full scholarship and went to New York University, explained, "No dreams = no goals = no plans = no future." Another senior, Sam, who earned enough to pay his tuition at UC Santa Barbara, added, **"Think about the future, but act right now."** The students finished their school work before they joined in extracurricular or social activities. Some used participation as motivation, since high grades must be maintained in order to take part. They also made wise choices in food (healthy over junk), music (not during study time), sleep (enough and on a regular schedule) and other daily activities and routines.

Shawn, a senior who was awarded a large scholarship to go to UC San Diego, set up a system of rewards and consequences for himself. He referred to the old example of the carrot and the stick. This wasn't some scheme imposed upon him by his parents. He created it himself. He enjoyed playing basketball with his friends, but only allowed himself to do so after his work was complete. He also hated doing yard work, and used it to punish himself when he missed a deadline.

Several graduates said they did what was beneficial for their future by making choices that would move them closer to reaching their goals. John, who later attended George Washington University, had to decide between two extracurricular activities. He chose tutoring music instead of playing a second sport because he rightly believed it would better fill out his college application.

Evelyn, who wanted to study veterinary medicine at UC Davis, decided to volunteer at a veterinary clinic during the summer instead of joining a swim team. Full-Ride students are determined to attain their objectives and make choices based upon this yardstick.

This same principle was used when making simple everyday decisions, like what to have for breakfast, and for more complex choices, like which enrichment course to enroll in during the summer. By using the same procedure, it became ingrained into their routines and eliminated stress and anxiety. They didn't worry about their choices, as they had a plan.

If they were ever confused, they sought help from their teachers or mentors. "In this life, we have to make many choices. Some are very important choices. Some aren't. The choices we make, however, determine to a large extent our happiness or our unhappiness, because we have to live with the consequences of our choices," James E. Faust, American religious leader, lawyer and politician.

## CHAPTER 16 - ACTION PLAN: (Parents until H.S., then Students)

List motivational items that could be put on display in bedroom; create vision board, "dream book" or hang college pennants.

## 17

## FOLLOW THROUGH

*"Doing the right thing isn't always easy – in fact, sometimes it's real hard – but just remember that doing the right thing is always right."*
*David Cottrell*

When I began sharing a few of the chapters from this guide with friends and family members, I experienced some push back. A few people lost sight of the way the information for this book was gathered. **The material was collected and collated from the real life experiences of hundreds of high school graduates.** None of it is theory. Present students and their parents will benefit from applying what was discovered when the habits of these scholarship winners were studied.

**My intention was to share what I discovered over several decades of teaching, and from the research I did on the success of scholarship applicants.** It was written so those who would rather receive more free cash for college instead of less would have a fighting chance to do so. After studying this guide, hopefuls will know what has worked for others. If they follow these examples, they will be more likely to graduate from college debt free.

After reading this book, individuals may be tempted to take shortcuts, but it makes no sense (or dollars) to do so. It would be simpler to eat a protein bar or drink a fruit smoothie instead of having a full meal for breakfast. But this isn't what those who earned the most scholarship money for college did. As explained in Chapter Five, those who completed their college education on other people's money instead of draining their parents' retirement funds or taking out thousands of dollars in student loans took the time to prepare and eat a complete, healthy breakfast daily.

I was told teenagers prefer to use their smart phones exclusively instead of also using flash cards or putting up white boards and calendars in their bedrooms. While this is obviously true for many, it isn't true of Full-Ride Scholarship recipients. Chapter Four goes into detail explaining how the graduates who received the most scholarship money did more than just use their smart phones.

Some families think it's beneficial for high schoolers to have a part time job each summer. They believe teens can earn college money this way. But no winner of a large scholarship in this study spent their summers doing so. They did, however, enroll in enrichment classes at various colleges and universities. Chapter Two goes into detail explaining what is essential in order to impress those who award college scholarships.

**The goal of this book is to enlighten those who want to know the "secret sauce" for obtaining significant college scholarships and grants.** Some really excellent students, with lots of promise, earned a much smaller amount in college scholarships or grants than others with less talent. This is because they failed to go beyond what is written in the college requirements guide. Those who do more become more and the colleges notice. They reward these applicants with more free cash for college. If going to college on a Full-Ride is the reader's goal, following this guide is a wise choice. As John Maxwell wrote, **"Successful people make their decisions based on where they want to be."** Remember, do more, be more and get more free cash for college.

For additional information on *Free College,* or other useful topics relating to education, go to my website, roadtofreecollege.com.

## CHAPTER 17 - ACTION PLAN: (Students)

Record fulfillment of all strategies listed in this book; all A — G requirements; Honors, AP, IB courses taken in areas of strength, talent or interest; extra foreign language, math or science courses taken.

# FREE COLLEGE

# Follow Through

# 18

## TIMELINE

*"Life is about timing."*
Carl Lewis

While it's indeed possible to ignore doing all the right things one should do in elementary and middle school and wait until the end of the ninth grade to begin setting goals and doing what is prudent; that's the hard way. It's far easier and better to develop effective habits at specific ages.

Below are two tables of the chapters in this book. They show the best times for children to begin developing the habits they contain (but, of course they should continue with them throughout high school). For ease of use, they're listed chronologically and by chapter.

Use this chart to know at what age you should begin the specific routine covered in each chapter. Refer to this section of the book whenever necessary in order to make the strategy a habit.

## CHRONOLOGY

| AGE | CHAPTERS | | | | |
|---|---|---|---|---|---|
| Pre-K | 1 | 5 | 14 | | |
| Elementary School | 3 | 4 | | | |
| Sixth Grade | 2 | 10 | 13 | 16 | |
| Ninth Grade | 6 | 7 | 9 | 11 | 12 | 15 |
| Tenth Grade | 8 | 17 | | | |

Use this chart when looking for the particular subject covered and the grade in which the practice contained therein is described.

**CHAPTERS**

| | SUBJECT | WHEN TO START |
|---|---|---|
| 1 | Do More, Be More, Get More | Pre-K |
| 2 | Take Enrichment Classes | Sixth grade |
| 3 | Take Music Lessons | Elementary school |
| 4 | Use Visual Aids | Elementary school |
| 5 | Eat Breakfast Daily | Pre-K |
| 6 | Start Looking Early | Ninth grade |
| 7 | Get Noticed | Ninth grade |
| 8 | Join Study Groups | Tenth grade |
| 9 | Focus | Ninth grade |
| 10 | Complete Every Assignment | Sixth grade |
| 11 | Ask Questions | Ninth grade |
| 12 | Befriend Competitive People | Ninth grade |
| 13 | Commit to Extracurricular Activities | Sixth grade |
| 14 | Dine as a Family | Pre-K |
| 15 | Find a Mentor | Ninth grade |
| 16 | Make Wise Choices | Sixth grade |
| 17 | Follow Through | Tenth grade |

## CHAPTER 18 - ACTION PLAN: (Parents, until H.S., then Students)

Record ACT/SAT test dates and scores, FAFSA deadlines, applications for college admittance, scholarships or grants; letters of recommendation, etc. Use lined pages following to record any information that exceeds the lined pages which follow each chapter.

# Timeline

# FREE COLLEGE

# Timeline

# FREE COLLEGE

# Notes

# FREE COLLEGE

# Notes

# FREE COLLEGE

# Notes

# FREE COLLEGE

# Notes

# FREE COLLEGE

# Notes

Made in the USA
Lexington, KY
01 July 2019